ANGLE OF YAW

BOOKS BY BEN LERNER

The Lichtenberg Figures
Angle of Yaw

ANGLE OF YAW

BEN LERNER

COPPER CANYON PRESS

Printed in the United States of America

Cover art: The protective cover of NASA's Voyager Golden Record. A 12-inch phonograph record, the gold-plated copper disc contains sounds and images selected to portray the diversity of life and culture on Earth.

Copper Canyon Press is in residence at Fort Worden State Park in Port Townsend, Washington, under the auspices of Centrum Foundation. Centrum is a gathering place for artists and creative thinkers from around the world, students of all ages and backgrounds, and audiences seeking extraordinary cultural enrichment.

LIBRARY OF CONGRESS CATALOGING-IN-PUBLICATION DATA
Lerner, Ben.
  Angle of yaw / Ben Lerner.
      p. cm.
  ISBN 1-55659-246-9 (pbk. : alk. paper)
  I. Title.
  PS3612.E68A84 2006
  811'.6—dc22

                        2006014260

COPPER CANYON PRESS
Post Office Box 271
Port Townsend, Washington 98368
www.coppercanyonpress.org

ACKNOWLEDGMENTS

Grateful acknowledgment is made to *Beloit Poetry Journal, Boston Review, Chain, Colorado Review, Common Knowledge, Conjunctions, Denver Quarterly, Jacket, jubilat, LIT, Passages North, The Poker, Provincetown Arts,* and *Revista de literatura hispánica,* where some of these poems first appeared.

Thank you, Ariana.

FOR MY PARENTS

FOR MY BROTHER

IN MEMORY OF ROSE

Printing, having found in the book a refuge in which to lead an autonomous existence, is pitilessly dragged out onto the street… If centuries ago it began gradually to lie down, passing from the upright inscription to the manuscript resting on sloping desks before finally taking to bed in the printed book, it now begins just as slowly to rise again from the ground. The newspaper is read more in the vertical than in the horizontal plane, while film and advertisement force the printed word entirely into the dictatorial perpendicular.

Walter Benjamin, "One-way Street"

*Frosted eyes there were that lifted altars;
And silent answers crept across the stars.*

Hart Crane, "At Melville's Tomb"

I

BEGETTING STADIA

I

for Marjorie Welish

Demands indefinitely specified,
demands incompatible with collective living

beget stadia
with indefinite seating
delicately tiered.

Resembling its shape
and therefore suggesting its function:

a wave.

Or repeating its shape
and therefore undoing its function:

a wave,

which I will here attempt to situate
in the broader cognitive process
of turning the page.

Just because these tears were on your face
doesn't mean they're yours.
The tree in your mind

is mine.
The redistribution of tears
reflects our collective commitment

to storm and stress,
to attitudes befitting participants in sports

and sports writing.
The conventions governing weeping in novels
do not apply to weeping done on-camera

or in teams.
Eldest sons dispossessed of ancestral tears
mock the tears of the nouveaux riches.
You call that weeping?

We call it sports entertainment
because the loser gets paid more,
because losing is hazardous,
because hazards are for losers

in the collective economy
of variable stars.

Rational actors wearing wrestling masks
would choose to lose collectively,
to collectivize losing
in the service industry.

I perform a valuable service
(I lose)
and I work from home.

Am I not then entitled to drink six beers
and watch some losing gracefully performed?

The sorcerer's apprentice is an animated mouse
losing control over water-toting brooms.
Now, what does that say about cleaning?

Sorcery cuts grease and glass like lightning!

Now, who will clean up this water?
What will we use to remove this water
from our jerseys? I suggest sorcery.

My Little League team is made up of animated mice
losing control of their jerseys
and delaying the game with lightning
in the manner of Fabius and Disney.

General Disney gets clothes clean (with sorcery).
General Disney's Chicken (with sorcery sauce).

The novel hurled to the ground breaks into verse
and achieves a perfect synthesis

of Bible and phonebook,
a chance synthesis
recalling the work of X
in its use of cherry and adverb.

A branch of adverb negatively rendered
is characteristic of a period
in which phonebooks possess all the qualities of epics

plus or minus three.
X is of that generation that gloried in synthesis
privately performed,
in charity syntheses held for cherry trees.

I have chopped down the truth conditions for cherry trees
with a chance synthesis,

with a phonebook in one hand
and a Bible in the other
and the other.

Configured to return to the thrower when hurled
and configured to return the thrower to the herd,

intended backfires configure warmth
for the polis and polis fans.
Context attributed to the skin at birth

picks teams:
shirts and skins,
redshirts and redskins
and tomahawking redskin fans.

"In 1825, the natives of Port Jackson hurled their halos and lay down."
Support your polis: chop the air.

The roof fell in
medias res.

We fled
into the trees.

But that part of
roof that was ceiling

that was glass,
we carry with us

here, he said,
touching his head

to his heart.
The roof fell in

in place and we
fled *here*

and *here,*
carrying our heads

in our hands,
holding our hands

to the light,
to that part of light

that was glass
and fell in

absentia.

II

ANGLE OF YAW

II

THE PREDICTABILITY OF THESE ROOMS is, in a word, exquisite. These rooms in a word. The moon is predictably exquisite, as is the view of the moon through the word. Nevertheless, we were hoping for less. Less space, less light. We were hoping to pay more, to be made to pay in public. We desire a flat, affected tone. A beware of dog on keep off grass. The glass ceiling is exquisite. Is it made of glass? No, glass.

THE BIRD'S-EYE VIEW abstracted from the bird. Cover me, says the soldier on the screen, I'm going in. We have the sense of being convinced, but of what? And by whom? The public is a hypothetical hole, a realm of pure disappearance, from which celestial matter explodes. I believe I can speak for everyone, begins the president, when I say famous last words.

ALL ACROSS AMERICA, from under- and aboveground, from burning buildings and deep wells, hijacked planes and collapsed mines, people are using their cell phones to call out, not for help or air or light, but for information.

IN THE EARLIEST FILMS, ACTORS PRETEND to accomplish prodigious acrobatic feats by rolling around on a black carpet while being filmed from above. The prophet who seems to ascend to heaven is being dragged across the floor. The first generation of moviegoers was unable to decipher the action on the screen, despite the *explicador.* The second generation mistook them for real grapes. In order to reproduce the colors of nature in our films, we have painted nature black and white. Startle the cuttlefish. Harvest the sepia. The literal color of fear.

ALL WE REMEMBER OF OUR CHILDHOOD is sliding down inclined chutes mounted by means of ladders, down slick chutes terminating in pools of water, across wet tarps laid atop the lawn, across hardwood floors in our socks, on short boards equipped with wheels, on roller skates, on ice skates, on ice, on gravel.

THE FIRST GAMING SYSTEM was the domesticated flame. Contemporary video games allow you to select the angle from which you view the action, inspiring a rash of high school massacres. Newer games, with their use of small strokes to simulate reflected light, are all but unintelligible to older players. We have abstracted airplanes from our simulators in the hope of manipulating flight as such. Game cheats, special codes that make your character invincible or rich, alter weather conditions or allow you to bypass a narrative stage, stand in relation to video games as prayer to reality. Children, if pushed, will attempt to inflict game cheats on the phenomenal world. Enter up, down, up, down, left, right, left, right, a, b, a, to tear open the sky. Left, left, b, b, to keep warm.

SHE WILL NEVER WANT FOR MONEY. Her uncle invented the room. On our first date, I told the one about the dead astronaut. How was I supposed to know? To prepare the air for her image, I put on soft music. I use gum to get the gum out of my hair. Like every exfoliated smear, we must either be stained or invisible. Maybe we should see other people? Impossible. The new trains don't touch their tracks. The new razors don't touch the cheek. If I want to want you, isn't that enough? No. Way too much.

HE HAD ENOUGH RESPECT FOR PAINTING to quit. Enough respect for quitting to paint. Enough respect for the figure to abstract. For abstraction to hint at the breast. For the breast to ask the model to leave. But I live here, says the model. And I respect that, says the painter. But I have enough respect for respect to insist. For insistence to turn the other cheek. For the other cheek to turn the other cheek. Hence I appear to be shaking my head *No*.

MINUTE PARTICLES OF DEBRIS IN SLOW DESCENT force evacuation of the concept. At what altitude does the view grow comprehensive? The daredevil places his head in the camera, eliciting oohs and aahs. We have willingly suspended our disbelief on strings in order to manipulate it from above.

IT IS WITH SOME DIFFIDENCE the author offers his public to the work. The tree remains where it was felled: inside the head, standing. For if my race provides an extensive field for theory, our rhymes are no less trash. The author retains no ill will toward the Gypsy people, nor a will in general. Without enthusiasm, we have chosen enthusiasm over truth. After dinner, straight to winter. Sidi Habismilk, I have searched the Internet. Nothing indicates your God is sorry. That's because our God is sorrow. In one palm, a lake of fire. In the other, a posthumous issue.

THE MASSIVE SWASTIKA, twenty meters in size, can only be seen from the air in autumn, when the larch trees turn a yellowish brown and stand out against the evergreen forest. Had the pattern been sown in the distant past, it would have been visible only to a higher being. At half-time, the marching band assumes a formation fully legible only to the blimp. But the blimp communicates the image of the field to a giant screen, allowing the crowd to perceive the flag formed by the musicians. The displacement of the horizontal plane by the vertical plane: the displacement of the God-term by the masses.

DEAR CYRUS, HE PUTS DOWN, DEAR CYRUS, yesterday
while taking the, he puts down, air in the company of M. de Charlus,
your cousin, the Baron, that is, while taking a spin, he puts down, in the
motorcar, which respects no mystery, to Thun, he puts down, to the town
of T, and the children trailing the, he puts down, which respects no, and
the children playing with smoke on a string, frozen smoke on a stick,
your cousin the Baron, drew my attention, my attention, you under-
stand, was drawn, there was a silver, and the children screaming, flying
machine, in terror, he puts down, with pleasure, and in the eyes of the
cousin, your Baron, who respects no, who is no, displayed like, longer,
objects, tears, of price, remain your, humble servant, I

THE PORTION OF THE STORY THAT REMAINS after the other components have been dissolved by churning. The woman attends the night game to watch the snow fall near the lights. Only the body of the protagonist is undergoing change. A whistle sweeps the town of meaning.

THE AVERAGE READER only perceives the initial and final letters of a word. He only reads the longest and most peculiar words in a sentence, intuiting the remaining language. The average reader often turns two pages at once, without perceiving a breach in narrative. He picks up a book, quickly flips through its pages, and believes it read. Conversely, he often reads unawares, will process and even vocalize a text he believes himself to be composing, while in fact reading skywriting, between the lines, on the wall. In your most intimate moments, my average reader, do you not rely on large cards held beyond the audience's sight? Have you ever applauded without being prompted by an illuminated sign?

THE PEOPLE'S REPUBLIC OF CHINA has launched a man into space. He claims the only man-made structure visible from the shuttle is the Great Wall. What about the Kansai International Airport (which is sinking)? The light from the Luxor Casino? What about smog? For *visible from space* read *in the eyes of God.*

THE PHENOMENA OF EXPERIENCE have been translated into understanding. Plug the exposed voids in the veneer cores to eliminate nesting. We live in the best of all possible worlds. Stain the compound to match the plywood finish.

THE AUTHOR EXPOSES HIMSELF IN PUBLIC like film. Every surface secretly desires to be ruled. A faint hazy cone in the plane of the ecliptic precedes the tabulation of a body by a train. Read only to resist the temptation to write. Skew lines and slickensides in an era of polarized light. The zip disk of snuff films your son defends as research has divided the community into infinite subdistances. Born losers born ready to be born again, we await the mayor's address in metal chairs. Then it hits me: I'm the mayor.

THE DOG IN THE CARTOON shoots a gun, overtakes the bullet in a car, and awaits it with an open mouth. Slight, continuous changes in the shapes of the scenery give the illusion of motion. In lieu of erections, sprouting cephalic contusions. Otherwise reduced to a pile of ash, the eyes of the mischievous cat remain, blinking. Contiguity substituted for substitution: flatten the duck with a frying pan and he becomes a frying pan. The bear indifferently fingers the holes in his chest. The giant ham around which the episode is organized weighs nothing, appears slippery, and is ultimately swallowed by a mouse. The popular breakfast sandwich is made of cartoon flesh. The child actor who worked opposite the drag-on is scarred for life. Open your eyes. You're still holding the dynamite.

NO MATTER HOW BIG YOU MAKE A TOY, a child will find a way to put it in his mouth. There is scarcely a piece of playground equipment that has not been inside a child's mouth. However, the object responsible for the greatest number of choking deaths, for adults as well as children, is the red balloon. Last year alone, every American choked to death on a red balloon.

NERVOUS EXHAUSTION FROM PROLONGED FLIGHT
cannot excuse her coloring. Nor that she was blinded at birth with a hot
wire to increase the beauty of her singing. A culture that lacks a concept
of lack remains foreign, no matter the quantity of aid, the quantity of cov-
erage. What do the homeless say in lieu of *Get out*? One day we will all be
landed. Remaining sensate into a late stage of decomposition, aka abstrac-
tion. Delivering supplies from the air is no problem. But to the air?

A WALL IS TORN DOWN to expand the room and we grow distant. At the reception, cookies left over from the intervention. In the era before the flood, you could speak in the second person. Now the sky-lighted forecourt is filled with plainclothesmen. I would like to draw your attention. Like a pistol? In the sense of a sketch? Both, she said, emphasizing nothing, if not emphasis. Squint, and the room dissolves into manageable triangles. Close your eyes completely and it reappears.

BEFORE THE INVENTION OF MOVIES, nobody moved. Rain like a curtain of beads. Snow like the absence of snow. Quit putting your mouth in my words, I said to the officer, before falling into his arms. Love of the uniform in lieu of uniform love. Lower your voice in a church, decrease your font in a poem. Not a sword suspended by a hair, but a mine triggered by a wire. At midnight, the question turns rhetorical. Does invention have a father? In an age of mechanical reproduction, is any sin original?

TO BUILD THE WORLD'S BIGGEST MIRROR, to outdate the moon, to dream en masse, to sleepmarch, to watch earthrise from the anonymous depths of our diamond helmets, screams Hamsun, and the general will will fall to the earth as highly stylized debris. For all that remains of the public are its enemies, whose image will not be returned, so let them eat astronaut ice cream, from which we have abstracted ice, let them read magazine verse in the waiting rooms of plastic surgeons commissioned to implant breasts into their brains. To pave the horizon with silver nitrate, to simulate the nation through reflected light, to watch over ourselves in our sleep, to experience mediacy immediately, screams Hamsun, raising his glass, by waking into a single dream, THE STATE.

A LARGE GROUP OF PICNICKING CHILDREN is struck by lightning. Four girls and four dogs are killed. Twenty-three children suffer burns, cataracts, macular holes, tympanic membrane rupture, and skull fracture. At the church service, the pastor organizes his eulogy around the trope of being called. God reached down with a finger of light, etc. But the positive charge originated in the ground and climbed an invisible ladder of electrons skyward.

THE PROSE IS DENSER than the plot, which pushes the plot to the surface. Walking around the hospital saying, People, we can do this. The style is rubbing off. Chicken again, or a satisfactory print thereof. It's amazing what we've accomplished, considering we're locked in the bathroom. It's OK to laugh. They can't hear you. Can you hear me? See: nothing.

THE ARTIST PROPOSES A SERIES OF LIGHTS attached to tall poles, spaced at intervals along our public roads, and illuminated from dusk to dawn. The public is outraged. The law's long arm cannot support its heavy hand. The public is outrage. Kindergartners simulate bayonet fighting with the common domestic fowl. Does this blood look good on me? Does this blood make me look fat? If you replace a cow's stomach with glass, don't complain when you cut your mouth.

READING IS IMPORTANT because it makes you look down, an expression of shame. When the page is shifted to a vertical plane, it becomes an advertisement, decree, and/or image of a missing pet or child. We say that texts displayed vertically are addressed to the public, while in fact, by failing to teach us the humility a common life requires, they convene a narcissistic mass. When you window-shop, when you shatter a store window, you see your own image in the glass.

WHEN NIGHT FALLS IN THE MIDDLE WEST we divide the multiple fruit of the pig. A drunk man calls out for traditional shepherds' music addressing the theme of love, scratch that, the theme of boredom. The children are made to recite the Office of the Shutting of the Eyes. The saltshaker is full of pepper. The peppershaker: glitter. At the bottom of every drained pool, there I are. There we am, openmouthed, awaiting the small, angular rain. A drunk man brews a second cup, one for each fist. Great tufts of white carpet pulled out in grief, scratch that, in boredom. In the planar region bounded by our counterglow, no means no. So does yes. Everything we own is designed to be easily washed, unlike the aprons of the butchers that we are.

WE DREAM OF RAIN that, in lieu of falling, moves parallel to the earth. Sheet after sheet of rain. Then an upward rain that originates a few feet off the ground. You can get under the rain and watch. With the disappearance of public space, we dream a rain that's moved indoors. A miniaturized rain restricted to one room, one wall, a box. Then we dream snow.

ONE WHO WOULD PURSUE a career as an assistant cannot be picky about what or whom she assists. Even the luckiest among us will spend years looking up precedents. In this we are ourselves assisted, usually by men who know nothing of surveying and have no tools. Shovel snow from the path; file snow under snow. We pursue our terminal degrees while watching somebody else's kids. The law student chases around the usher's wife. The inspector laughs because you're laughing. Not having read the author in question is no defense against the charge of plagiarism. Our boss is the hushed tone in which we discuss him.

THE PUBLIC DEPENDS upon private sorrow. Well-regulated peacetime sorrow. I respect no office founded before the invention of the pistol, before an emphasis on brushstroke. We decide on a motion. The body vetoes. Nostalgia is futurity's privileged form in this economy of downturns. Is the television a linear descendant of the musket or the hearth? In American motels, the lamps are nailed down so that you will want to steal them, a Christian notion. Get off my property, she says, when I try to calm her down. Get out of my car, she says, when I try to wake her up. We stop our rotten teeth with gold. We drink a crystal cola. We counteract unwanted odor at inestimable human cost. As if you could choose between loving and leaving the weather. The rich kids in Providence are moving to Mexico. Rich kids in Mexico are moving to Providence. I'm on my umpteenth Pabst, awaiting order, making difference.

RETURNING ASTRONAUTS almost always fall into a deep depression. They are stricken with an uncontrollable desire to gain weight. At dusk you will see them circling the park in silk pajamas, mocked by children, trailed by dogs. Prolonged weightlessness destroys the bones, the muscles, and, eventually, the larynx, which is why when astronauts return to earth we find that their speech has been reduced to a kind of quiet piping, at once soft and shrill, that is intelligible only to other astronauts, a piping that approaches, but is not, despite the government's assertions, song.

IF IT HANGS FROM THE WALL, it's a painting. If it rests on the floor, it's a sculpture. If it's very big or very small, it's conceptual. If it forms part of the wall, if it forms part of the floor, it's architecture. If you have to buy a ticket, it's modern. If you are already inside it and you have to pay to get out of it, it's more modern. If you can be inside it without paying, it's a trap. If it moves, it's outmoded. If you have to look up, it's religious. If you have to look down, it's realistic. If it's been sold, it's site-specific. If, in order to see it, you have to pass through a metal detector, it's public.

WE ARE A MEAN AND STUPID PEOPLE, but not without smooth muscle. When we get offended, we say, What's the big idea. The rest of the time we don't worry about it. Instead of national genius, a native lyric twined around the latticework of grammar. The bees we sent to space stopped making honey. Like a grown man, the monkeys wept. The night the shuttle crumbled on reentry, you were allowed to hug anybody you could find. We just stretched out on the beach. Best night of our lives.

A WELL-PLACED BLOW TO THE TEMPLE and it's 1986 in aeternum. Like a kid in a candy store crossed with a bull in a china shop, a depressive in a garage. After your uncle hooks you up, a sudden inability to recall where you got your doctorate, let alone in what. Walking around the basement asking, Whose blood is this? Not the beauty of the bottle rocket, but its justice. The infinite sympathy of breakaway glass. Bro, you said that already. Another summer spent searching for something to nurse back to health. Finding yourself.

THE GIRL PLAYS with nonrepresentational dolls. Her games are devoid of any narrative content, amusements that depend upon their own intrinsic form. If you make her a present of a toy, she will discard it and play with the box. And yet she will only play with a box that once contained a toy. Her favorite toy was a notion about color. She lost it in the snow.

THE DETECTIVE pushes red tacks into the map to indicate where bodies have been found. The shooter is aware of this practice and begins to arrange the bodies, and thus the tacks, into a pattern that resembles a smiley face. The shooter intends to mock the detective, who he knows will be forced to confront this pattern daily on the precinct wall. However, the formal demands of the smiley face increasingly limit the shooter's area of operation. The detective knows, and the shooter knows the detective knows, that the shooter must complete the upward curving of the mouth. The detective patrols the area of the town in which bodies must be found if the shooter is to realize his project. The plane on which the killings are represented, and the plane on which the killings take place, have merged in the minds of the detective and the shooter. The shooter dreams of pushing a red tack into the map, not of putting a bullet into a body. The detective begins to conceive of the town as a representation of the map. He drives metal stakes into the ground to indicate the tacks.

WE WORK IN ACCOUNTING for taste. True, Mallarmé wasted a lot of paper, but less than your average American. Liner notes eclipse the music, like eating the rind and discarding the flesh. How many Indians remain on the fence, they asked her, to see if she were gifted, then locked her in the closet with a carton of smokes. From the land's natural depressions arises the affect of home. Where the lines break of their own accord. Where shockwaves pulverize our stones. Let the machine get it, she was wont to say, when we didn't have a phone.

THE CAMERA WAS DISCOVERED before painting was invented. The first paintings were made on the inside walls of cameras. Still, painting was the first medium to attain a verisimilitude capable of confusing birds, the highest achievement in any art. When Wu Daozi painted dragons, their fins stirred. The rest of the story is about flatness. One-sided surfaces. A skin that speaks a vocabulary of rights. To explore color, we realized, leave it out. Like exchanging genius for its stroke. The bald girl is interested in boredom. I'm interested in algal cells and fungal hyphae. Our grant is awarded in installments of cigarettes. We are trying too hard not to be funny.

THE GOOD AND EVIL, THE BEAUTIFUL AND UGLY, have been assumed under the rubric of the interesting. Non sequitur rendered lyric by a retrospective act of will. Tongue worries tooth. Repetition worries referent. Non sequitur rendered will by a retrospective act of lyric.

HIDEAWAY BEDS were not invented to maximize space, but to conceal the unseemly reality of prostration. Thomas Jefferson, who held the first United States patent on a hideaway bed, devised a system of elevating and securing the bed to the ceiling. Each night the bed would be lowered slowly, and with great ceremony, thereby associating the animal fact of sleep with the plane of the divine. The contemporary hideaway bed, which is stored vertically, has snapped shut and killed at least ten businessmen. Most people can be trained to sleep standing up, to sleep with their eyes open, to somniloquize, to somnambulate. Mobilizing this tremendous dormant workforce is an ancient dream. Astronauts sleep strapped to their beds, like lunatics, like the lunatics they are.

PEOPLE WITH ALL MANNER OF PHOBIA, a fear of heights or crowds or marketplaces, public speaking or blood or prime numbers, have been known to overcome their panic by wearing glasses, not with corrective lenses, but with lenses of plain shatterproof plastic, which not only impose a mediate plane between them and the object of their fear, but apply a comforting pressure to the bridge of the nose. When you encounter a person seized by terror, softly squeeze this bony structure, and he will be instantaneously subdued. In an age of contact lenses and laser surgery, it is safe to assume that a person who persists in wearing glasses is undergoing treatment.

A BACHELOR made from a cake of shaving soap and a tin of denti-frice, pursued by an admiring throng of whiskers and teeth, announces a willful deadness of surface called *publicity*. The animate talks back to the animator, blowing his cover as delicately as glass. A poorly painted explosion either resembles a bunch of flowers (static) or a nosebleed (overly rich in color); the brushstroke itself must be made to mime the direction of the pressure. When our story opens, gas begins to stream. The crowd yawns with wonder. History, screams Hamsun, the junior senator from Wisconsin, will vindicate my mustache. When a vanguard in bowlers mows down a vanguard in tarbooshes, you've reached modernity; leave a message at the beep.

LASER TECHNOLOGY has fulfilled our people's ancient dream of a blade so fine that the person it cuts in half remains standing and alive until he moves and cleaves. Until we move, none of us can be sure that we have not already been cut in half, or in many pieces, by a blade of light. It is safest to assume that our throats have already been slit, that the slightest alteration in our postures will cause the painless severance of our heads.

A SIDE OF BEEF ON A SILVER PLATTER, a slice of life on a silver screen. A beast with two backs, a war with two fronts. *Búsqueda en Google* an Abraham doll with realistic trembling. Her exit is emphasized by the receding lines of the parquet floor—who says art criticism is impractical? I'll grant the world doesn't need another novel, if you'll grant the novel doesn't need another world. The smugness masks a higher sadness, a sudden chiasmic reversal mistaken for love. I just want to be held, but contingently, the way the mind holds a trauma that failed to take place. Realistic suction, realism sucks. Ah, Bartleby!

III

DIDACTIC ELEGY

III

Sense that sees itself is spirit

Novalis

Intention draws a bold, black line across an otherwise white field.
Speculation establishes gradations of darkness
where there are none, allowing the critic to posit narrative time.
I posit the critic to distance myself from intention, a despicable affect.
Yet intention is necessary if the field is to be understood as an economy.

By *economy* I mean that the field is apprehension in its idle form.
The eye constitutes any disturbance in the field as an object.
This is the grammatical function of the eye. To distinguish between objects,
the eye assigns value where there is none.

When there is only one object the eye is anxious.
Anxiety here is comic; it provokes amusement in the body.
The critic experiences amusement as a financial return.

It is easy to apply a continuous black mark to the surface of a primed canvas.
It is difficult to perceive the marks without assigning them value.
The critic argues that this difficulty itself is the subject of the drawing.
Perhaps, but to speak here of a subject is to risk affirming
intention where there is none.

It is no argument that the critic knows the artist personally.
Even if the artist is a known quantity, interpretation is an open struggle.
An artwork aware of this struggle is charged with negativity.
And yet naming negativity destroys it.
Can this process be made the subject of a poem?

No,
but it can be made the object of a poem.
Just as the violation of the line amplifies the whiteness of the field,
so a poem can seek out a figure of its own impossibility.
But when the meaning of such a figure becomes fixed, it is a mere positivity.

Events extraneous to the work, however, can unfix the meaning of its figures,
thereby recharging it negatively. For example,
if airplanes crash into towers and those towers collapse,
there is an ensuing reassignation of value.
Those works of art enduringly susceptible to radical revaluations are masterpieces.
The phrase *unfinished masterpiece* is redundant.

Now the critic feels a new anxiety in the presence of the drawing.
Anxiety here is tragic; it inspires a feeling of irrelevance.
The critic experiences irrelevance as a loss of capital.

To the critic, the black line has become simply a black line.
What was once a gesture of negativity has lost its capacity to refer
to the difficulties inherent in reference.
Can this process be made the subject of a poem?

No,
but a poem may prefigure its own irrelevance,
thereby staying relevant
despite the transpiration of extraneous events.

This poem will lose its relevance if and when there is a significant resurgence
of confidence in the function of the artwork.
If artworks are no longer required to account for their own status,
this poem's figures will then be fixed and meaningless.

But meaninglessness, when accepted, can be beautiful
in the way the Greeks were beautiful
when they accepted death.
Only in this sense can a poem be heroic.
After the towers collapsed

many men and women were described as heroes.
The first men and women described as heroes were in the towers.
To call them heroes, however, implies that they were willing to accept their deaths.
But then why did some men and women
jump from the towers as the towers collapsed?
One man, captured on tape, flapped his arms as he fell.

Rescue workers who died attempting to save the men and women trapped in the towers
are, in fact, heroes,
but the meaning of their deaths is susceptible to radical revaluation.
The hero makes a masterpiece of dying
and even if the hero is a known quantity
there is an open struggle over the meaning of her death. According to the president,

any American who continues her life as if the towers had not collapsed
is a hero. This is to conflate the negative with the counterfactual.
The president's statement is meaningless
unless to be American means to embrace one's death,
which is possible.

It is difficult to differentiate between the collapse of the towers
and the image of the towers collapsing.
The influence of images is often stronger than the influence of events,
as the film of Pollock painting is more influential than Pollock's paintings.

But as it is repeated, the power of an image diminishes,
producing anxiety and a symbolic reinvestment.
The image may then be assigned value where there is none.
Can an image be heroic?

No,
but an image may proclaim its distance from the event it ostensibly depicts;
that is, it may declare itself its own event,
and thereby ban all further investment.

The critic watches the image of the towers collapsing.
She remembers less and less about the towers collapsing
each time she watches the image of the towers collapsing.

The critic feels guilty viewing the image like a work of art,
but guilt here stems from an error of cognition,
as the critic fails to distinguish between an event
and the event of the event's image.

The image of the towers collapsing is a work of art
and, like all works of art, may be rejected
for soiling that which it ostensibly depicts. As a general rule,
if a representation of the towers collapsing
may be repeated, it is unrealistic.

Formalism is the belief that the eye does violence to the object it apprehends.
All formalisms are therefore sad.
A negative formalism acknowledges the violence intrinsic to its method.
Formalism is therefore a practice, not an essence.

For example, a syllogism subjected to a system of substitutions
allows us to apprehend the experience of logic
at logic's expense.

Negative formalisms catalyze an experience of structure.
The experience of structure is sad,
but, by revealing the contingency of content,
it authorizes hope.

This is the role of the artwork—to authorize hope,
but the very condition of possibility for this hope is the impossibility of its fulfillment.
The value of hope is that it has no use value.
Hope is the saddest of formalisms.

The critic's gaze is a polemic without object
and only seeks a surface
upon which to unfold its own internal contradictions.
Conditions permitting, a drawing might then be significant,
but only as a function of her search for significance.

It is not that the significance is mere appearance.
The significance is real but impermanent.
Indeed, the mere appearance of significance is significant.
We call it *politics.*

The lyric is a stellar condition.
The relation between the lyric I and the lyric poem
is like the relation between a star and starlight.
The poem and the I are never identical and their distance may be measured in time.
Some lyric poems become visible long after their origins have ceased to exist.

The heavens are anachronistic. Similarly, the lyric
lags behind the subjectivity it aspires to express. Expressing this disconnect
is the task of the negative lyric,
which does not exist.

If and when the negative lyric exists, it will be repetitious.
It will be designed to collapse in advance, producing an image
that transmits the impossibility of transmission. This familiar gesture,
like a bold black stroke against a white field,
will emphasize flatness, which is a failure of emphasis.

The critic repeats herself for emphasis.
But, since repetition emphasizes only the failure of sense,
this is a contradiction.
When contradictions are intended they grow lyrical
and the absence of the I is felt as a presence.

If and when the negative lyric exists, it will affect a flatness
to no effect.
The failure of flatness will be an expression of depth.

Towers collapse didactically.
When a tower collapses in practice it also collapses in theory.
Brief dynamic events then carry meanings
that demand memorials,
vertical memorials at peace with negativity.

Should we memorialize the towers or the towers' collapse?
Can any memorial improve on the elegance of absence?
Or perhaps, in memoriam, we should destroy something else.

I think that we should draw a bold, black line across an otherwise white field
and keep discussion of its meaning to a minimum.
If we can close the event to further interpretation
we can keep the collapse from becoming a masterpiece.

The key is to intend as little as possible in the act of memorialization.
By intending as little as possible we refuse to assign value where there is none.
Violence is not yet modern; it fails to acknowledge the limitations of its medium.
When violence becomes aware of its mediacy and loses its object
it will begin to resemble love.
Love is negative because it dissolves
all particulars into an experience of form.
Refusing to assign meaning to an event is to interpret it lovingly.

The meaninglessness of the drawing is therefore meaningful
and the failure to seek out value is heroic.
Is this all that remains of poetry?

Ignorance that sees itself is elegy.

IV

ANGLE OF YAW

IV

THE DARK CROWD CANNOT BE SEEN DIRECTLY, the dark crowd does not interact with light, but the dark crowd can be detected by measuring its gravitational effects on visible crowds. The visible crowd moves toward the dark crowd, as insects toward a black-light trap, in the tropism we call *history*. Riot guns with rubber bullets, tear gas, water cannons, flying wedges of heavily armored police, are not only incapable of dispersing the dark crowd, but, by inciting a phase change in the visible crowd, expand its ranks.

SEEN FROM ABOVE, exposition, climax, and denouement all take place at once. God sees the future as we see the past: through a trimetrogon. In the name of the camera, the film, and the view itself. Simultaneous eternities are superimposed to create the illusion of plenitude, but the transposition of planes is a poor substitute for the transmigration of souls. I think Andrei Rublev says, *Nothing is as terrible as snow falling in a temple*, because without a distinction between inside and outside, there can be no extra-temporal redemption. That, and how anybody can just lie down and make an angel, even a Tartar. Even an angel.

A PERSON IS PHOBIC, that is, mentally imbalanced, when his fears fail to cancel out his other fears. The healthy, too, are terrified of heights, but equally terrified of depths, as terrified of dark as light, open spaces as closed. The phobic are overbold, not overly apprehensive, and must be conditioned to fear the opposite of what they fear. The difficulty of such a treatment lies in finding the counterbalancing terror. What is the opposite of a marketplace? A prime number? Blood? A spider?

TALK ME DOWN, MAN, TALK ME DOWN. Obsessive repetition
of meaningless gestures. A dangerous level of light in the blood. The
caller claims to have discovered the imprint of a trilobite embedded in
the sky. It's the kind of thing, he says, that makes you pray to God. That
you might live forever. In these several states of shock. At what point in
the conversation did you realize her breathing had stopped? When I
kissed her. But there's no time for this. The black helicopters are upon us,
our daughters flee from the house, weeping, crazy with joy.

AN IMAGE OF ULTIMACY in an age of polarized light. Will you marry me, skywrites the uncle. A pill to induce awe with a side effect of labor. A lateral inward tilting and the aircraft pushes its envelope. A minor innovation in steering outdates a branch of literature. Envelopes push back. The way a wake turns to ice, then vapor, then paper, uniting our analogues in error, intimacy's highest form. Jet engines are designed to sublimate stray birds. *No* appears in the corn.

THE THIRD DIVISION OF A RUMINANT'S STOMACH is called a *psalterium* because, when slit open, its folds fall apart like the leaves of a book. The fruit is star-shaped when cut in cross section and is therefore called *star fruit*. Our people often name an object after the manner in which we destroy it.

THE VIEWING PUBLIC DEMANDS an image of itself. The revelation of a telltale trope. The evidence is against us, rubbing. Heat from the right margin reduces the sentence. Light, dry, explosive snow. The pianist is remembered for his influential humming over what is considered a poor rendition. Of radical emotional incapacitation. Of opaque, damp permutation. At what point did you kick away the ladder? In chapter four, where the reader is encouraged to look down from above. Where the author, posing as a question, opens up the floor.

I BELIEVE THERE IS A QUESTION IN THE BACK. Yes, thank you. Do you own Hitler's upper teeth? If you do own Hitler's upper teeth, and it seems that you do, would you be able to resist the temptation to try them on? If you're wearing Hitler's upper teeth right now, and it seems that you are, how does that effect the validity of your answer? What if you write your answer? If you tell me you love me while wearing Hitler's upper teeth, should I believe you? Is it wrong to be kissed by a person wearing Hitler's upper teeth? What if the person wearing the teeth is Jewish, a rabbi even? Can we put a dollar figure on the upper teeth of Hitler? Are the upper teeth of every German in some important sense the upper teeth of Hitler? Would it be a good or bad thing for German children to be forced to try on the upper teeth of Hitler? And if it would be a good thing, and I think we can all agree that it would, is that because they would learn that these teeth are somehow exceptional, maybe even supernatural, or because they would realize that Hitler's upper teeth are composed of a soft pulp core surrounded by a layer of hard dentin coated with enamel—just plain old teeth? Can Hitler's upper teeth ever be forgiven? And, if so, all at once?

ONE IF BY LAND, TWO IF BY SEA, sings the canary. Warning: coloration. The very existence of concealed space constitutes an ambush. An abrupt change in sentence structure turns our fire friendly. Our response is calculated to make a false alarm come true, a true alarm come false. There is no describing a weapon that spreads white space.

WOMEN HAVE NO DESIRE to travel in outer space. When men have forced women to travel in outer space, the results have been disastrous. If you mention space travel to a woman, she will say, Don't even go there, she will say, You can't go home again, she will say, Been there, done that. That there is more space inside one small woman than in all of heaven has been verified experimentally. She will say, Have I gained weight, she will say, I no longer love you and/or I'm not sure I ever loved you, she will say, Most theorists believe the universe is flat. The first woman in space is still there.

DEAR CYRUS, HE PUTS DOWN, DEAR CYRUS, what you experience as an inconsistency in tone, is, in fact, the Montessori method, in which we practice abstinence during the period of ovulation, in which we move across the plane of fracture, where adjacent surfaces are differentially displaced. Dear Personified Abstraction, he puts down, Dear Counterstain with Safranine, I am writing to describe a perfect circle, the sudden sine curve of a fleeing deer, and to request your absence at my table, with quakes of lesser magnitude to follow. Dear Reader, he puts down, Dear He Puts Down, when the golden parachute failed to decelerate your cousin, the Baron, the first dog in space, the kids fanned out across the field and screamed *I've got it,* mistaking the shower of sparks for bedtime, the luminous obligate parasites for a lecture on film. Dear Lerner, he puts down, Earth to Lerner, throw three damn strikes and get us out of this sentence, but the runner had long since grown into his base.

CHILD ACTORS are not children, that much we know. Their reputation for viciousness is, by all accounts, deserved. Napoleon and Liszt were child actors. In situation comedies, child actors are black. Some child actors have never been off-camera. If you build a set and start filming, a child actor will come downstairs. Some doctors believe it is the constant surveillance that stunts the growth of the child actor, the pressure of the viewing public's gaze, while in fact a child actor off-camera is like a fish out of water. He cannot breathe.

WE HAVE ASSEMBLED for the athletic contest in tiered seats. Once, we assembled in a central core with mobile spiral arms. Or, lying on our backs, we formed a radiating cluster, imposing animal figures and names upon the stars. Now we watch heavily armored professionals assume formations on a grid of artificial grass. Wishbone. Shotgun. Power I.

WE CAN FEEL THE CHANGING of the tense. The sky distends six inches. Like a parachute opening inside the body. If you don't secure your own mask first, you'll just sit there stroking the child's hair. In the dream you form part of the wreckage you pick through: an allegory of reading. Who knows how many hijackers have been foiled by an engrossing in-flight movie. This one seems to be about symmetry, about getting yours. Its simplified geometrical forms recall the landscapes of our simulators. It's not just the pilots who have to be trained. When you ask the stewardess for another tiny bottle, she says, This is neither a time nor a place.

PHOTOGRAPHED FROM ABOVE, the shadows of the soldiers seem to stand upright, casting bodies. Birds are rarely depicted from a bird's-eye view. From this angle, she doesn't love me. Half light, half ideology. Each of us is impressed as pixels into an ad for democracy. Give the people what they want, says the TV. A powerful suction effect? Extra-extra-cheese? The sixth sense, the sense with which we read, is the ability to perceive the loss of other senses; we have lost this sense.

THE SMUGNESS MASKS A HIGHER SADNESS. We are unaware of the patterns we generate. In the carpet grass, the snow crust. When we don't know a word, we say, Look it up. Up? And the Lord withdrew his thumb, trailing delicate, rootlike filaments, leaving a hole in my chest the size of a polis. From which I address you, Hamsun. If you dig deep enough, you hit water, then hell, then China. So why not fly? Getting there is half the fun; the other half: not getting there.

A SUDDEN EXPERIENCE OF STRUCTURE and the heart gives out. He checks himself in. Lies on the window and looks out the bed. The sense of having said it before keeps him, again and again, from beginning. As the belief that the respirator is powered by the rain keeps him breathing. The outlet is inhabited by a family of mice who also regard their home as a source of power. He shuts his eyes to see himself from above. He shuts his eyes so tightly they recoil. To be forced to drink water is an ancient form of torture, older than being denied water. That the body eats itself is neither here nor there. With what exceeds description we busy ourselves.

THIS IS NOT YOUR FATHER'S BOREDOM. 1986: the year in pictures, the year in tears. Out of the ordinary emerged the first, doomed shoots. In my honor they will one day name and electrify a chair. Wind in my hair, windshield in my teeth. A grammar derived for an early death. Mere wit is the new wailing; black, the new black. My best friend went to Mexico and all I got was this lousy elegy. As easy as taking context from a baby. I'd like to say a few words in memory of Memory, an all-state wrestler who left teeth-marks on the median. I can't help feeling that it should have been me. It was, whispers the priest.

AS LONG AS THE BREATH LASTS, the vowel can be pro-
longed. The name refers both to the field of play and the game itself, in
which you can utilize any part of the body save the brain. A flat, affected
tone is sweeping the nation. We sincerely hope we will never have to use
the cables strung to the scenery, but it's nice to know they're there.

A STUDY OF A CHILD [ERASED], a study of erasure [Child], the swiftness of pencils repeating a theme until it achieves the illusion of enterable space. Rake me, she said, with a moral light, but the luster of her ostrich-feather fan had dimmed her eyes. For the purposes of study, we have removed those figures attributed to disciples, yielding a string of visual commas and the inscription *Turn away*. We work with a found vocabulary, working backwards from the detail to the richly textured blindness of Parmigianino's gaze. Anyway, as a child, I was thrown from my Powell Peralta, and when I came to, my left-brain had been erased. No street, no land, no sky—just scape.

WE ARE PLEASED TO OFFER A LAMP that turns on and off when you clap, when you clap your eyes. A lamp that lets you see in the dark without disturbing the dark. A lamp producing natural light. A lamp that when you clap turns on and on.

IN THE COMMERCIAL she just stabs a straw into an orange and sucks. We tried that at home and lost massive amounts of blood. When I was little, she confessed, beginning to cry, we were forced to race in sacks, to race in pairs with our near legs bound. Coach was finally fired for rewarding each good hit with a sparkling article of porn. His slow-pitch team was sponsored by AA. His house was always already egged. It was when I tried to eat a straw through a straw that I learned my first important lesson about form.

WHEN WE FOUND EYES in the hospital Dumpster, we decided to build the most awesome snowman ever. The author addresses the reader; the clown, the kids at home. Angels are absences in the snow, visible only from above. When it thaws they will stand up and search for the children they have known.

THE ROSE has a minutely serrate margin, like a poem. There ends analogy. A dying process. At the border of the cornea and sclera, a momentary wavering. Excluded from beatific vision, but not condemned to further punishment. In the dream she told me she felt fine. Like dust. To what shall we liken analogy, if not to hypermetropia. These carpets are the color of migraine. Note to self: change your life. I assume the palmate antlers of hoofed mammals have so often been likened to candelabra I'm not even going to try. Boy, you got trouble in your head. Every time, he says, breasts are described in the poems of men, a woman undergoes mastectomy. I said *he says* to gain some credibility, which is a privileged form of distance. This one goes out to Grandma Elsie, short for Elsewhere, whom I never met. This one goes out to Grandma Rosie, who couldn't remember her first cancer by the time she died of being ready. Her ashes are on a shelf in Cambridge. Awaiting scattering. Note to self: don't publish this. Besides the half-dead and their families, everybody in the home was from the Indies. Carpets the color of. We administered music and morphine. For ninety-four years, she had performed her gender admirably. Anyway, this isn't a time or a place. But the day she died some punk nearly hit me with his bike, parked it, and got all in my face. Boy, you got trouble in your head. I started to cry. Like a woman, he said. As if to give me strength.

WE BEG THE QUESTION that gives the lie. Which swallows the usage. Half of the panel supports the sentence: Without emotion. We pursue a color of maximum lightness. Town crier become town drunk. A diet of bacon and meth. Prolonged speech making to delay the action. Of the hammer. Convicted on the strength of his indifference to conviction. The music is inadmissible. The gavel fell on a percussion cap and now we're holding candles, singing, My God, My God, show me what you're working with.

RAPIDLY REPEATED STIMULI have locked our jaws and fixed our gazes upward. Public launches are designed to trick the body into an attitude of prayer. Despair is an oculogyric crisis, as every politician knows, and can be treated with displays of strength in the upper air. Perhaps scratching out one's eyes is all that remains of bearing witness, but note the hegemony of the image among the blind. The way our national uncle stares from the poster, claiming to want every passerby. *Nunc dimittis servum tuum,* you murderers. I come from a long line of prematurely balding communards who would prefer not to. Keep your infernal, infertile high ground, with its toll roads of crushed glass.

A GREAT BOOK must be frozen and fractured along its faults in order to lay bare internal structure. Anna Karenina touches the paperknife to her cheek. When a child dies in a novel, he enters the world. And writes the novel. The calories in a great book equal those burned in its reading. Or its burning. Even if there are no great books, argues Levin, we must act as if there were. For the sake of the peasants who work the paper. A gentleman may fight duels only with other gentlemen. A reader may not demand satisfaction.

A BRIEF, COLLECTIVE SHUDDER and the desire passed into its opposite. The public shared a cigarette. Now to choose between loving our offspring and loving offspring in general, between veiling the reference and taking the vow. The right to have it both ways is inalienable or it isn't. You can't have it both ways. A contradiction shifting planes produces lightning. Or a reflection of distant lightning in the clouds.

THE MAN OBSERVES THE ACTION ON THE FIELD with the tiny television he brought to the stadium. He is topless, painted gold, bewigged. His exaggerated foam index finger indicates the giant screen upon which his own image is now displayed, a model of fanaticism. He watches the image of his watching the image on his portable TV on his portable TV. He suddenly stands with arms upraised and initiates the wave that will consume him.

EQUIPPED WITH FLUFFY PLUMAGE that allows for almost noiseless flight. Our bombs are dropped from such altitudes our wars have ended by the time they reach their targets. Like that sentence. No, like any sentence. Maintaining the blood supply to the brain during rapid vertical acceleration requires subtle reasoning, soft music. Hence an earphone in the helmet. What goes up, must come down, pleads the child of the astronaut. Not if you go way, way up.

A SURGERY TO ABRIDGE the body. A reader-friendly body pre-sented to the public. The public depends from a well-regulated militia. Our army, too, has its required reading. A soldier must read Tolstoy's *War* (abr.), Dostoyevsky's *Crime* (abr.). Even in death, the old debate between depth and surface: some poets attach weights to their ankles, others just float facedown. What is the value of reading? Depends. What is it keep-ing you from doing?

AN INFINITE PROGRESSION OF FINAL FRONTIERS
designed to distract the public from its chest wound. We will not just sit
here being mooned, insists the president. Your kids are arranging a day
of national mourning with a trunk full of tequila and pipe bombs. In
despair, the painter returns to the figure. Or has the world grown
abstract? In my experience, the eyeball hardens. In my opinion, the
sound of weeping. Maybe the microphone itself is speaking. On the
count of three, everyone everywhere concede everything.

THE INHERENT DIFFICULTY OF THE GAME rests exclusively in the obscurity of its object. Points are taken away for killing civilians, but points are irrelevant. Gold earns you extra men. Children, if questioned, deny the mediation of the joystick or fail to hear the question. Often we are permitted to return to levels we've surpassed to search for mushrooms.

THE TIME-RELEASE SEDATIVE is advertised by means of accelerated photographic frames. The music fails to produce conscious awareness but evokes a violent response. As an artist I'm interested in filling things with blood, especially clocks, but as a mom I demand the illusion of continuous motion. Best viewed through radial slits in a drum. Best viewed before 1987. A flickering series of stills induced by a stroke in turn induces a stroke, restoring the illusion of continuous perceptual flow. My colleagues, what have we learned? That consciousness has a neural correlate in snow. That movement is painted on.

SHE HAS TAPED AN AERIAL PHOTOGRAPH of our neighborhood to the ceiling. She looks up to see our house from above while we're in bed. This is but one example of her uncontrollable desire to look down on the structures that she's in.

AMERICANS HAVE CONQUERED THEIR FEAR of public speaking by abolishing the public. Chief among our exports: wisps of precipitation. Because it receives the impression of your teeth, it is genuine emotion. Compare the streak left on the gemstone with that left on the retina. Confusing the desire to display affection with affection, we applaud the veterans of an imaginary conflict with real victims. An immoderate reverence for tradition guides everything but our reading. I throw my own party and go away.

THE SOLDIER IN THE FILM asks the audience to describe his wounds. Unaware his legs are elsewhere, he attempts to walk out of the screen. What matters is the form, not the content, of the airdrop, how it alludes to manna. Then kill me, he begs. Active soldiers act like actors, inactive actors act like soldiers, audience members vomit in their giant sodas. Dance, I say, aiming near his feet. Think, I say, aiming near his head. The crowd dismembers. Now I'm on my back, making an angel, awaiting not the peanut butter and propaganda, but the flowering apparatus that retards its fall.

SPUN DOWN FROM AND REELED UP TO the hand by a flick of the wrist. In what sense is it a toy, she asks, if it catches real fish? Like soldiers carrying popguns and switchblade combs. At first, the elephant could fly only when he held a feather in his trunk. Would you rather live during the ascension of a civilization, asks the top-hatted cricket, or during its decline? Pygmalion or Pinocchio? Then he learned to hold it in his mind. Not every off-screen voice is the voice of God. But we must act as if it were. For the sake of the rabbit who has run out of landscape and plugged the shotgun with his finger. Do rabbits have fingers? I don't know, do chickens? The hunted confounds the hunter with a sudden change of gender.

THE TONE DOES TERRIBLE THINGS to the landscape. Its flatness drapes the landscape in unspeakable light, unspeakable space. The public, delicately inflamed, attempts to change the channel. But a channel cannot be changed by force. During the course of festive occasions, ash rains down. Bits of parti-colored ash inform us that our tone is festive. Perhaps change must come from within a channel, suggests Levin, from within a landscape draped with depth?

DEAR CYRUS, HE PUTS DOWN, DEAR REPETITION, while you were driving home from, how shall I put this, Mexico, driving dark pales into the panic grass, the kids got into the Roman candles, the ginger vodka, the Bible I gave your daughter was hollow, contained a, how shall I, pistol, two kinds of people in this world, do I smell incense, swimmers and nonswimmers, a child with puppy dog eyes asks if puppies go to heaven, the pistol proves untrainable, ruins the carpet, a no or no question, I guess I just assumed dogs dog-paddled, Dear, Dear, he puts down, Dear Me, when a dog drowns an angel gets its wings, and a long proboscis for sucking blood, no self-putdowns, she screamed, I pretended it was alive so I could pretend to put it to sleep, how shall I, sweetheart, no doggy heaven, put this, without a doggy hell.

HOLD ME, says the microphone. The dialogue inside my body is breaking down. The doctor insists on changing the tense, but the gesture is lost on me, stranded on the skin. When did I ever say that I could teach you how to live, demands the canvas. Light wishes only to be a history of its transfers, wishes only to be land. They have pricked my back with a series of suspected allergens, an allegory of reading, but my skin is notoriously indifferent. To print media. To the dialogue of fear and pity designed to restore the public's settings. You have a swelled head, complain my hands.

THE SUN SETS IN A WEAK SENSE, striking conjunctions of rock from the view, imparting a vivid red to the red to the red—the text is skipping. The author dreams of cutting an adjective and tucking it behind the reader's ear like a flower. And cutting *like a flower* and tucking it behind the reader's ear like a flower.

BORN NOSTALGIC, THE ARTIST PROPOSES a return to despair. He installs himself in your freezer. The critic argues it is not real hair, that real hair could never do this. At what point, asks the critic, did you realize the blood was fake? About halfway through the transfusion, when he began to talk a bunch of bullshit. About the formal capacity for choice? Yes, how did you know? I worked as an artist during the war.

THE AIRCRAFT ROTATES about its longitudinal axis, shifting the equinoxes slowly west. Our system of measure is anchored by the apparent daily motion of stars that no longer exist. When the reader comes to, the writer hits him again. Just in case God isn't dead, our astronauts carry sidearms. This is not your captain speaking, thinks the captain. A magnetic field reversal turns our fire friendly. Fleeing populations leave their bread unleavened, their lines unbroken.

WHEN WE SAW THE PATTERN, we took the kids out of school. Broke out the special water. Two churches linked by a sudden alley through the corn. As the Hopi myth foretells. A massive loss of technology. A spider leaves a string between two points. Think about it. From the duster it appears a thing of glory. Makes you reconsider the whole idea of property. Stems inside formations have blown nodes. Explain that, Mr. TV. Part of the confusion involves words. We wake up with mud on our feet. The other part is just the way we are. Scared of the new when it's thousands of years old. If you have never seen a sleeping toddler crawl beyond the lip of porch light, zip it. If my meaning is clear, it's already too late. For God's sake people. Open your hearts.

V

TWENTY-ONE GUN SALUTE FOR RONALD REAGAN

V

I am wearing a Mikhail Gorbachev Halloween mask.
Blood is a vegetable when it forms part of a school lunch.
Tell the boys to go out there and win one for me.
The former president entered my room at night.
We celebrated by breaking off pieces of the wall.
I want the tone to have a very broad surface in relation to its depth.
I want a gun for protection.

 I want the form to enact the numbing it describes.
 I would shoot myself only in self-defense.

Pornography considered as a weapon system and v.v.
An accurate Civil War reenactment should include reinstating the draft.
The stigma attached to a diplomatically communicated disease.
It's important to talk to your readers about drugs.
The nipple is just visible under the anchorwoman's blouse.
This is your tax dollars hard at work.
I have deleted many beautiful lines.

 A highly accurate weapon housed in a silo.
 I can't stop crying.

I was drunk the night of the accident.
All the other painters were like, Why didn't I think of that?
I have agreed not to defend Poland from the east.
I have agreed not to defend Poland from the East.
Mom says we can keep it if we feed it.
Nightlights go out all over America.
Brutus is urging his comrades to seize a fleeting opportunity.

 We salivate at the sound of the bell.
 That part of the concept corresponding to the wrist

is slit, emitting music.
There go the conventions Dad gave his life to protect.
The Soviet director argued convincingly against the use of sound.
Characterized by alternating rigidity and extreme flexibility.
The president's legacy is speaking slowly.
An epistemology borrowed from game shows.
Love is made to highly realistic dolls.
>The passivity of dolphins has been wildly exaggerated.
>Abortion is murder.

A child could have painted that.
We dipped cicadas in WD-40 and ignited them with punks.
Magnetic resonance imaging reveals a degenerate hemisphere.
A diamond cheval-de-frise tops the White House.
The floral arrangement is based on outmoded ideology.
I am unmatched in my portrayal of subtle human emotions.
Workers report cracks in our mode.
>There is no beauty like the beauty of a throwaway line
>the split second before it's thrown.

We carried home the reader shoulder high.
I neither regret nor recall my presidency.
Carefully equilibrated parts designed to move in the breath.
It can easily be converted into a fully automatic.
Mikey likes it.
I prefer apostasy from the top down to belief from the bottom up.
You must cross four bases in a diamond pattern in order to score.
>The bang caused by the shockwave
>preceding an aircraft traveling at the speed of sound

is my middle name.

I am attempting to stress the absence of hope while implying resignation.

A trademark used in a figurative context and in lowercase.

Minute hooks fasten to a corresponding strip with a surface of uncut pile.

A moment of unprecedented clarity experienced as a loss.

The starlings nesting in the bell's flared opening

did not hear the toll that slew them.

     This is a masterpiece on a very grand scale.

     I have drastically relaxed the standards of sexual behavior.

The pathos is visible when you hold the poem to the light.

She comes twice a month, in the first and third quarters of the moon.

The Soviets have prevailed.

I am beloved for my hoarse voice, ample nose, and timeworn hat.

The silvery leaves change position at nightfall.

What if we start over underground?

I propose truth is reached by a continuing dialectic.

     I disagree.

     Your life isn't worth the paper it's printed on.

My practical designs include a 1934 Sears refrigerator

and the interiors of NASA spacecraft.

Infinite Mind; Spirit; Soul; Principle; Life; Truth; Love.

An ideal cage bird given the pronounced affection among mates.

I am fond of lightning without audible thunder.

Reach out and touch someone.

Even the most conservative among us have lost all faith

     in the possibility of evoking a common cultural framework.

     Nobody moves

and nobody gets hurt.
The stoatlike creature symbolizes guilt.
The meanings detonate at preset depths.
I have never felt like a real man.
The holocaust is advanced tentatively to test public reaction.
Weeping is substantially, but not technically,
an admission of wrongdoing.

       Flight attendant: Oh my God, Oh my God, Oh my—
       Control tower: Take deep breaths.

A quick search has turned up the appropriate affect.
I respect the silky detail of your still-life paintings.
If you had been hypnotized, silly, you wouldn't know it.
This way the reader can answer other incoming calls.
Proceeds from the arms sales were then funneled to the Contras.
They held my father down and shaved his beard.
America is the A-team among nations,

       bursting with energy, courage, and determination.
       May I put my tongue in your ear?

Never wake a sleepwalker.
The Orient has regained the lamp and we are doomed.
Such a process of repetition is called reduplication.
The passion to be reckoned upon is fear.
The audience hears the voice of an on-screen character
who is not seen speaking.
These angels will eat anything—demon, sparrow, angel.

       My ability to appeal to white Southerners
       has diminished considerably

since I posed nude in the pages of *Foreign Policy*.
My government dropped an aluminum soap of various fatty acids
on my pen pal and her family.
Why don't we blame the sinking on Spain?
Financial benefits accorded to big business will be passed down to consumers.
Reading is cool.
A little shadow enhances the memory.

> We conduct ourselves in a free and easy manner
>
> but at heart are false and cold.

"God Bless America" was memorably sung by Kate Smith.
They were married hours before their double suicide.
You never called me before I was famous.
The names of the dead are inscribed in the wall.
The play is making Hamlet's mother uncomfortable.
I can't feel my legs.
The limit of latitude past which trees will not grow.

> Tear down this wall.
>
> Let them eat snow.

Then, without warning, our guiding star burned out.
We stood around the sleeping infant to see if she was breathing.
The poet notes that beautiful days and seasons do not last.
My emergence from my mother was captured on film.
All I ask is that we stop executing the mentally handicapped.
The stadium lights prevent the cereus from blooming.
But what if the mentally handicapped want to be executed?

> Big Bird towers over the human actors.
>
> We have both the right and duty to expand

into the blasted lands of southwest Asia.
Let's add touches of ethnic instrumentation.
I am attracted to women I do not respect.
The child makes a substantial advancement in poetics
with a canister of hair spray and a Bic.
Then you wake up next to a war criminal.
A rapid slide through a series of consecutive tones.
        The memorial will have to be continuous.
        Lift every voice and sing.

Your brother told me he feels mostly dead on the inside.
The strings are damped by wood and metal.
Station signals, picked up by elevated antennas
are delivered by cable to the receivers of subscribers.
Sexual abstinence is a partial solution.
A vague but strong attraction draws me to Moscow.
The white prizefighter doesn't have a prayer.
        Entities should not be multiplied needlessly.
        I can get you a healthy baby for five hundred dollars.

It's a lot better if you take out the plot.
Silvered surfaces face the vacuum.
The nightingale filled the pauses between sobs.
Mechanically separated chicken parts.
Crocodiles weep to attract victims.
There are such moments in life, dear reader, such feelings…
One can but point to them—and pass them by.
        All that remains of pleasure is frottage.
        The clouds were sown with crystals of dry ice

to stimulate rain for the president's funeral.
Private-sector affluence, public-sector squalor.
The hostage is growing romantically attached to her captor.
Jesus likes me.
My visit to the dermatologist possessed a nightmarish quality.
Mercy, the speaker is instructing Shylock, must be given freely.
Then this girl stood up.

> She couldn't have been more than sixteen.
> What if we just stop killing people

no matter our reasons?
Mathematics and literature are antagonistic cultures.
The camera moves steadily on the dolly.
Tempered to break into rounded grains instead of jagged shards.
I orbited the earth forty-eight times aboard *Vostok 6.*
A term for dreamless sleep no longer in scientific use.
What about the love, she asked,

> the love, the love
> the love?

People were laughing and booing.
The studio manager was waving his arms.
The candidate said something about the road to hell.
Updates are ready to install.
Splash paint to achieve a spontaneous effect.
Children gain pleasure from both passing and withholding.
Oyez, oyez, oyez.

> They slipped the surly bonds of earth and touched the face of God.
> Is this thing on?

ABOUT THE AUTHOR

Ben Lerner is from Topeka, Kansas. He holds degrees in political theory and creative writing from Brown University. His first book, *The Lichtenberg Figures,* won the 2003 Hayden Carruth Award and was named by *Library Journal* one of the twelve best books of poetry published in 2004. A former Fulbright Scholar to Spain, Lerner co-founded and co-edits *No: a journal of the arts.* His poems can be found in a variety of literary magazines, including *Boston Review, Colorado Review, Conjunctions, Fence, The Paris Review, Piedra de molina* (Madrid), and *Ploughshares.* He lives in Berkeley.

The Chinese character for poetry is made up of two parts: "word" and "temple." It also serves as pressmark for Copper Canyon Press.

Founded in 1972, Copper Canyon Press remains dedicated to publishing poetry exclusively, from Nobel laureates to new and emerging authors. The Press thrives with the generous patronage of readers, writers, booksellers, librarians, teachers, students, and funders—everyone who shares the conviction that poetry invigorates the language and sharpens our appreciation of the world.

Major funding has been provided by:
Anonymous
The Paul G. Allen Family Foundation
Lannan Foundation
National Endowment for the Arts
Washington State Arts Commission

Copper Canyon gratefully acknowledges
Madeleine Wilde, whose generous Annual Fund
support made publication of this book possible.

For information and catalogs:
COPPER CANYON PRESS
Post Office Box 271
Port Townsend, Washington 98368
360-385-4925
www.coppercanyonpress.org

This book was designed by Phil Kovacevich using the typefaces Bank Gothic for headings and Minion for the text. Bank Gothic was designed in 1930 by Morris Fuller Benton for American Type Founders. Minion was designed in 1992 by Robert Slimbach for Adobe Systems.

Printed in the USA
CPSIA information can be obtained
at www.ICGtesting.com
JSHW050540270823
47298JS00001B/2

9 781556 592461